CW00558742

A LITTLE BIT OF
TAYLOR SWIFT

summersdale

AN UNOFFICIAL
CELEBRATION OF
A MODERN ICON

An Hachette UK Company
www.hachette.co.uk

Summersdale Publishers
Part of Octopus Publishing Group Limited
Carmelite House
50 Victoria Embankment
LONDON
EC4Y 0DZ
UK

www.summersdale.com

Printed and bound in Poland

ISBN: 978-1-83799-590-5

This FSC® label means that materials used for the product have been responsibly sourced

MIX
Paper | Supporting responsible forestry
FSC® C018236

Substantial discounts on bulk quantities of Summersdale books are available to corporations, professional associations and other organizations. For details contact general enquiries: telephone: +44 (0) 1243 771107 or email: enquiries@summersdale.com.

This book is unofficial and is not endorsed by or in any other way connected with Taylor Swift – it is written for Swifties by Swifties. Every effort has been made to ensure that all information is correct. Should there be any errors, we apologize and shall be pleased to make the appropriate amendments in any future editions.

TO

....

FROM

....

INTRODUCTION

Dear reader,

Whether Taylor is your role model, your greatest hero or the soundtrack to your life, all your wildest dreams are about to come true! Exploring her extraordinary journey from a small-town girl to one of the most successful and empowered artists of the twenty-first century, this is your backstage pass to the enchanting world of Taylor Swift.

Take on the Taylor trivia to become a certified Swiftie, find your new life motto in her words of wisdom, and where her personal life and career are concerned, get to know her better with facts that will give you a front-row seat.

A Little Bit of Taylor Swift is a heartfelt homage to Taylor, her loyal fans and our enduring love story, one that will become folklore for Swifties everywhere, for evermore.

…Ready for it?

OTHER WOMEN WHO ARE KILLING IT SHOULD

MOTIVATE YOU, THRILL YOU, CHALLENGE YOU AND INSPIRE YOU.

TAYLOR SWIFT

Taylor's CD lyric booklets contain hidden messages. Across her first four albums, the seemingly random capitalized letters actually spell words or phrases, ranging from named subjects to more cryptic hints. And just to keep us Swiftie sleuths on our toes, Taylor did the opposite in her album *1989*, using uncapitalized letters as a code.

According to the Pet Rich List 2023, what is the estimated net worth of Taylor's cat, Olivia Benson?

---

a) $13 million

b) $65 million

c) $97 million

IF YOU'RE
BEING MET WITH
RESISTANCE,
THAT PROBABLY
MEANS THAT
YOU'RE DOING
SOMETHING NEW.

TAYLOR SWIFT

DID
YOU
KNOW...

Taylor almost had a tax named after her! In 2015, the government of Rhode Island proposed a luxury tax on any second home in the state that was valued at over $1 million. Inspired by Taylor's $17.75 million purchase of her famous Rhode Island beach house, High Watch, the charge was nicknamed the "Taylor Swift tax" – although in the end it wasn't passed.

Taylor wrote her first song when she was just 12 years old and only knew how to play three guitar chords (C, D and G). What was it called?

_____

a) "I'd Lie"

b) "Lucky You"

c) "Tim McGraw"

Grow a backbone, trust your gut and know when to strike back.

TAYLOR SWIFT

DID YOU KNOW...

Taylor reserves a special spot on her albums for her heartbreak anthems. Did you really think it was a coincidence that such tear-jerkers as "Dear John", "All Too Well", "my tears ricochet" and "So Long, London" all occupy the fifth spot on their respective tracklists?!

From a series of ethereal *folklore* gowns to a snake-themed catsuit for *Reputation*, Taylor's jaw-dropping wardrobe played a starring role in her record-breaking Eras Tour, documented in the concert film of the same name. But just how many costume changes were there during the performance?

a) 10

b) 13

c) 16

NO MATTER WHAT LOVE THROWS AT YOU, YOU HAVE TO BELIEVE IN IT.

YOU HAVE TO BELIEVE IN LOVE STORIES AND PRINCE CHARMINGS AND HAPPILY EVER AFTER.

TAYLOR SWIFT

DID YOU KNOW...

While Taylor is known for leaving clues in her work to hint at her upcoming plans, she once planted a red herring for her fans. The night before the 66th Annual Grammy Awards, Taylor changed all her social media profile pictures to black and white, leading the world to believe that *Reputation (Taylor's Version)* would be announced, only to surprise us all with a brand-new album: *The Tortured Poets Department*.

The *1989* track
"Welcome to New York"
was featured in which of
these animated movies?

———

a) *Soul*

b) *Bolt*

c) *The Secret
Life of Pets*

APOLOGIZING
WHEN YOU HAVE
HURT SOMEONE
WHO REALLY
MATTERS TO YOU
TAKES NOTHING
AWAY FROM YOU.

TAYLOR SWIFT

DID YOU KNOW...

It's no secret that Taylor wrote the fan favourite "Enchanted" with Adam Young from Owl City in mind – but did you know that he actually covered the song in reply? In 2011, Adam wrote Taylor a letter and shared it on his Tumblr page before recording his own version of the song to let her know that he was "Enchanted" to meet her, too!

Who is the only featured artist on Taylor's eighth studio album, *folklore*?

---

a) The National

b) Bon Iver

c) The Civil Wars

The only real
risk is being too
afraid to take
a risk at all.

TAYLOR SWIFT

DID
YOU
KNOW...

Taylor was named after the
singer-songwriter James Taylor,
and not just because he was one
of her parents' favourite artists.
They also believed that a gender-
neutral name would help Taylor
forge a career in any area in which
women were underrepresented,
especially in business.

Known for her tight-knit friendship group, Taylor is a girl's girl. But which of these friends directed the music video for "I Bet You Think About Me (Taylor's Version) (From the Vault)"?

a) Lena Dunham

b) Blake Lively

c) Selena Gomez

MUSIC IS THE ONLY THING THAT'S EVER FIT ME LIKE THAT

LITTLE BLACK DRESS YOU WEAR EVERY SINGLE TIME YOU GO OUT.

TAYLOR SWIFT

DID
YOU
KNOW...

In the music video for "Look What You Made Me Do", Taylor bathes in a tub of diamonds rather than cash. Swifties speculate that the single dollar bill visible in the shot represents the symbolic $1 in damages she was awarded when she won a sexual assault trial against a former radio DJ in 2017.

We all remember the fedora and those iconic heart-shaped glasses, but what was the slogan on Taylor's T-shirt in the music video for "22"?

———

a) Junior Jewels

b) Not a lot going on at the moment

c) I ♥ NY

THERE ARE TWO
WAYS YOU CAN GET
THROUGH PAIN. YOU
CAN LET IT DESTROY
YOU, OR YOU CAN
USE IT AS FUEL
TO DRIVE YOU:
TO DREAM BIGGER,
WORK HARDER.

TAYLOR SWIFT

DID YOU KNOW...

If you were to enjoy a night out
with Taylor, her drink of choice
would be a chilled vodka and
Diet Coke. Alternatively, if you
went to a drive-thru instead,
she would order a cheeseburger,
fries and a chocolate milkshake.

Which classic novel
inspired the *evermore*
track "tolerate it"?

---

a) *Rebecca*
by Daphne du Maurier

b) *Wuthering Heights*
by Emily Brontë

c) *Pride and Prejudice*
by Jane Austen

There are so
many different
things that you
can discover
about yourself
if you write.

TAYLOR SWIFT

DID
YOU
KNOW...

At only 14 years old, Taylor was
talent-spotted by record executive
Scott Borchetta when she performed
at a listening room in Nashville.
Taylor was one of the first artists
to sign with Borchetta's new,
independent record label Big Machine
Records and released her debut
album in October 2006. A year later,
it had sold over one million copies.

Which of these movies does
Taylor *not* appear in?

———————

a) *Amsterdam*

b) *Valentine's Day*

c) *Monte Carlo*

NO MATTER WHAT HAPPENS IN LIFE, BE GOOD TO PEOPLE.

BEING GOOD TO PEOPLE IS A WONDERFUL LEGACY TO LEAVE BEHIND.

TAYLOR SWIFT

DID
YOU
KNOW...

In 2019, Taylor turned her
philanthropist efforts to supporting
the LGBTQ+ community. She began
a petition to send the Equality
Act to the President's desk so it
could be brought up for a vote in
the Senate. She drew attention
to this petition by referencing it
in her Pride-themed music video
for "You Need to Calm Down".

Which song did Taylor write
for her band, The Agency?

_____

a) "Long Live"

b) "Change"

c) "I'm Only Me When
I'm With You"

IT'S THE MOST
MADDENING, BEAUTIFUL,
MAGICAL, HORRIBLE,
PAINFUL, WONDERFUL,
JOYOUS THING IN
THE WORLD, LOVE.

TAYLOR SWIFT

DID YOU KNOW...

Blake Lively and Ryan Reynolds's children feature in Taylor's songs. Their names – James, Betty and Inez – are referenced in the album *folklore*, and James's voice introduces the *Reputation* track "Gorgeous", for which she received credit in the lyric booklet.

In 2022, Taylor was awarded
an honorary doctorate
in fine arts from which
American university?

_____

a) Yale

b) NYU

c) Harvard

You are your
own definition
of beautiful and
worthwhile.

TAYLOR SWIFT

DID
YOU
KNOW...

The lyrics or melodies of Taylor's songs sometimes come to her in dreams. As soon as she wakes up, she either records herself singing on her phone or scribbles her ideas down. Taylor revealed in an interview that the *1989* track "All You Had to Do Was Stay" came about this way.

Which band starred
in the music video
for "Bejeweled"?

a) HAIM

b) The Chicks

c) Fifth Harmony

WITH EVERY
REINVENTION,
I NEVER WANTED
TO TEAR DOWN
MY HOUSE.

'CAUSE I BUILT
THIS HOUSE.

TAYLOR SWIFT

Thirteen isn't Taylor's lucky number simply because she was born on the thirteenth. Taylor has experienced a lot of synchronicity with the number: her first number-one hit, "Tim McGraw", had a 13-second introduction, and her first record went Gold in 13 weeks. She even wrote the number 13 on her guitar-strumming hand before her concerts for many years.

Which of these stars did *not* make a guest appearance in the music video for "Bad Blood"?

———

a) Hayley Williams

b) Lana Del Rey

c) Ellie Goulding

A LOT OF THE
BEST THINGS I EVER
DID CREATIVELY
WERE THINGS THAT
I HAD TO REALLY
FIGHT – AND I MEAN
AGGRESSIVELY FIGHT
– TO HAVE HAPPEN.

TAYLOR SWIFT

The invisible string Taylor refers to in
the *folklore* track of the same name
is drawn from an East Asian folk
myth about the red thread of fate,
a red-coloured string that joins two
soulmates together across time and
space. Taylor also used this imagery
in the music video for "willow".

Taylor updated an infamously controversial lyric when she released her version of *Speak Now*. On which track can you find this new lyric?

_____

a) "Superman (Taylor's Version)"

b) "Better Than Revenge (Taylor's Version)"

c) "The Story of Us (Taylor's Version)"

People haven't
always been
there for me,
but music
always has.

TAYLOR SWIFT

Taylor is the queen of the cat eye
and has admitted that she once used
a Sharpie in an airplane toilet when
she didn't have any eyeliner to hand.
She does, however, strongly advise
any fan against following suit.

Taylor underwent an impressive physical transformation for her role in the music video for "The Man", donning prosthetics, heavy make-up and even a muscle suit. But who played the voice of Taylor's male alter ego?

———

a) Leonardo DiCaprio

b) Dwayne Johnson

c) Ryan Gosling

EVERY ONE OF MY REGRETS HAS PRODUCED

A SONG THAT I'M PROUD OF.

TAYLOR SWIFT

DID
YOU
KNOW...

While Taylor wrote many of her
earliest songs on her bedroom
floor, she co-wrote "Everything
Has Changed" with Ed Sheeran
while they were bouncing on
her garden trampoline.

Which track on *Fearless* was
inspired by Taylor's best
friend from high school?

———

a) "The Best Day"

b) "Fifteen"

c) "Hey Stephen"

ONE THING
ABOUT LEARNING
TO BE THE BEST
FRIEND YOU
CAN POSSIBLY
BE IS KNOWING
WHEN TO LET
PEOPLE FIGURE
THINGS OUT ON
THEIR OWN.

TAYLOR SWIFT

Taylor loves hugs. When she sported a $9,000 Oscar de la Renta fairytale floral minidress – and a matching face covering – to the 63rd Annual Grammy Awards, a seam ripped under her right arm during the evening. Magazines will tell you this probably happened as she celebrated her win with her collaborators, but Swifties speculate the malfunction was from hugging people too tightly.

Which of these tracks opens
with the sound of sirens?

———————

a) "I Did Something Bad"

b) "Getaway Car"

c) "no body, no crime"

You have
to write 100
songs before
you write the
first good one.

TAYLOR SWIFT

DID
YOU
KNOW...

Taylor has a unique, previously secret way of categorizing her music. She revealed via Apple Music and Spotify playlists that she thinks of her songs as "Quill Pen", "Fountain Pen" or "Glitter Gel Pen" songs, according to the mood of the lyrics.

Which of these tracks *only*
appeared on *Midnights
(The Til Dawn Edition)*?

a) "Bigger Than
the Whole Sky"

b) "Hits Different"

c) "The Great War"

**YOU MAY
LEAVE BEHIND
FRIENDSHIPS
ALONG THE WAY,**

**BUT YOU'LL
ALWAYS KEEP
THE MEMORIES.**

TAYLOR SWIFT

Taylor grew up on an 11-acre
Christmas tree farm in Reading,
Pennsylvania. One of her jobs was
to pick praying mantis egg pods
off the trees and rehome them in
the forest before the trees were
sold to customers – a detail which
unsurprisingly does not feature on her
2019 single "Christmas Tree Farm"!

What was the
first single released
from Taylor's seventh
studio album, *Lover*?

―――――――

a) "You Need to
Calm Down"

b) "Cruel Summer"

c) "ME!"

YOU ARE NOT
GOING NOWHERE
JUST BECAUSE
YOU ARE NOT
WHERE YOU WANT
TO BE YET.

TAYLOR SWIFT

DID
YOU
KNOW...

A now-iconic blue guitar embellished with koi fish inlays accompanied Taylor on the Speak Now World Tour from 2011 to 2012. Ever the mastermind, Taylor released her rerecording of *Speak Now* over a decade later on 7 July – National Koi Day.

How many copies did
the album *1989* sell
in its first week?

———————

a) 1,180,000

b) 1,240,000

c) 1,280,000

You are the
only one
who gets to
decide what
you will be
remembered for.

TAYLOR SWIFT

Three tracks on the album
folklore are actually part of the
same story; "cardigan", "august"
and "betty" are told from the
perspectives of three individuals
and tell the tale of a summer
affair. Taylor refers to this trilogy
as "The Teenage Love Triangle".

Which of these songs
was *not* a vault track on
Fearless (Taylor's Version)?

———————

a) "Mr. Perfectly Fine"

b) "Untouchable"

c) "We Were Happy"

TRYING AND FAILING AND

TRYING AGAIN AND FAILING AGAIN IS NORMAL.

TAYLOR SWIFT

For many years Taylor wore glasses or contact lenses to correct her near-sightedness (her prescription was -1.5) until she underwent LASIK eye surgery. Her mum recorded Taylor recovering from the anaesthesia, and the hilarious footage became an instant meme: "I'm not asleep, my mind is alive!"

Which track was written specifically about Taylor's disillusionment with American politics following the 2018 US midterm elections?

___

a) "Only the Young"

b) "Miss Americana & the Heartbreak Prince"

c) "You Need to Calm Down"

BANISH THE DRAMA.
YOU ONLY HAVE
SO MUCH ROOM
IN YOUR LIFE
AND SO MUCH
ENERGY TO GIVE
TO THOSE IN IT.
BE DISCERNING.

TAYLOR SWIFT

DID
YOU
KNOW...

After winning a radio network talent show in 1950, Taylor's grandmother Marjorie Finlay toured on the show *Music With the Girls*. The opera singer inspired Taylor to pursue a career in music. The *evermore* track "marjorie" actually features Finlay's soprano as the backing vocals.

Which of these artists was *not* a surprise guest on the Reputation Stadium Tour?

———

a) Bryan Adams

b) Sara Bareilles

c) Niall Horan

Never forget
the essence of
your spark!

TAYLOR SWIFT

Taylor's music has a number of country influences, especially charismatic female performers who are known for their moxie. These include Shania Twain, The Chicks and, of course, LeAnn Rimes, who was Taylor's childhood hero because she started her music career at just 13.

Which track on
Reputation is allegedly
about Taylor's relationship
with Tom Hiddleston?

a) "Don't Blame Me"

b) "Getaway Car"

c) "This Is Why We Can't
Have Nice Things"

I LOVE WRITING
SONGS BECAUSE I
LOVE PRESERVING
MEMORIES,

LIKE PUTTING A
PICTURE FRAME
AROUND A FEELING
YOU ONCE HAD.

TAYLOR SWIFT

DID YOU KNOW...

While Taylor has had some famous collaborators during the years, including Aaron Dessner and Jack Antonoff, she wrote *all* the songs on *Speak Now* by herself, aged just 19. This was in response to critics who had speculated that she hadn't written her own music on her two previous albums.

Taylor's career-spanning Eras Tour featured a staggering 44 set songs and two surprise acoustic songs, and the show ran for over three hours. But what was the first song on the Eras Tour setlist?

---

a) "Lover"

b) "...Ready For It?"

c) "Miss Americana & the Heartbreak Prince"

I THINK IT'S
IMPORTANT THAT
YOU KNOW THAT
I WILL NEVER
CHANGE. BUT I'LL
NEVER STAY THE
SAME EITHER.

TAYLOR SWIFT

DID
YOU
KNOW...

Taylor has actually framed a
photograph of the moment that
Kanye West notoriously hijacked
her acceptance speech for Best
Female Video at the 2009 VMAs.
It hangs in the living room of
her Nashville duplex, above a
handwritten caption that reads:
"Life is full of little interruptions."

Which of Taylor's cats
stars in the music video
for "Blank Space"?

_____

a) Meredith Grey

b) Olivia Benson

c) Benjamin Button

I'm always afraid of failing. I have to quiet that fear if I'm going to get up in the morning.

TAYLOR SWIFT

DID YOU KNOW...

Taylor wrote and performed the hit single "Our Song" for her ninth-grade talent show! Little did she know that with that very same song, she would become the youngest person to ever write and sing a number-one country single on the Hot Country Songs chart.

When was Taylor's
tenth studio album,
Midnights, released?

a) April 2021

b) October 2022

c) July 2023

GIVING UP DOESN'T ALWAYS MEAN YOU'RE WEAK.

SOMETIMES YOU'RE JUST STRONG ENOUGH TO LET GO.

TAYLOR SWIFT

You can study Taylor Swift at university! Stanford University, Arizona State University, the University of Ghent and Queen Mary University of London were the first to offer modules that analyse Taylor's career and cultural impact, and in 2023 the University of Melbourne in Australia even held Swiftposium, a three-day Taylor-themed academic conference.

Which of these tracks was *not* written about one of Taylor's grandparents?

___

a) "Mary's Song"

b) "epiphany"

c) "marjorie"

I'M THANKFUL
THAT WHEN I GO
TO BED AT NIGHT,
THAT I HAVE BEEN
MYSELF THAT DAY.
AND I HAVE BEEN
MYSELF ALL THE
DAYS BEFORE THAT.

TAYLOR SWIFT

DID
YOU
KNOW...

The *Fearless* track "Love Story"
isn't just special because it is
a fairytale fan favourite. It was
actually the first song to ever reach
number one in the US – in both the
pop *and* country music charts.

Which was the first album Taylor owned the master recordings to?

---

a) *Fearless (Taylor's Version)*

b) *Lover*

c) *folklore*

I'm intimidated
by the fear of
being average.

TAYLOR SWIFT

Taylor has explained that she may
never perform the track "Soon You'll
Get Better". She wrote the song
about her mother's battle with cancer,
and she felt that performing it would
make her too emotional. She did
however perform a piano solo of the
track for the television special *One
World: Together at Home* during
the Covid-19 pandemic where the
song took on a different meaning.

What ambient sound
features on the tracks
"exile" and "evermore"?

---

a) birdsong

b) rainfall

c) waves

PEOPLE ARE GOING TO JUDGE YOU ANYWAY,

SO YOU MIGHT AS WELL DO WHAT YOU WANT.

TAYLOR SWIFT

DID YOU KNOW...

Taylor has taken the world by storm with the rerecordings of her first six albums. In 2019, a talent manager acquired the rights to her master recordings and sold them on – a transaction which allegedly took place behind her back and despite the fact she wanted to buy them herself. She rerecorded her albums in order to own the full copyright to her work.

What was the 2020 Netflix original autobiographical documentary about Taylor's career and songwriting process called?

———————

a) *Miss America*

b) *Miss Americana*

c) *America's Sweetheart*

WE LIVE IN A
WORLD WHERE
ANYONE CAN SAY
ANYTHING THAT
THEY WANT ABOUT
YOU AT ANY TIME.
BUT JUST PLEASE
REMEMBER THAT
YOU HAVE THE
RIGHT TO PROVE
THEM WRONG.

TAYLOR SWIFT

DID YOU KNOW...

Taylor originally titled her seventh studio album *Daylight*. However, she felt this might be too on the nose given the tonal shift from her previous, darker album, *Reputation*, so she instead chose *Lover*.

In the *1989* track "Wonderland", what colour are the love interest's eyes?

_____

a) blue

b) brown

c) green

Never believe
anyone who
tells you that
you don't
deserve what
you want.

TAYLOR SWIFT

DID YOU KNOW...

When she was 14, Taylor spent the summer writing a young adult novel which she titled *A Girl Named Girl*. Taylor's parents still have a copy of the manuscript, and Taylor has since trademarked the title, suggesting that she might be reserving it for a future project...

Taylor's mythical "lost album", which she allegedly replaced with *Reputation*, is said to have been titled what?

___

a) *Comeback*

b) *Vendetta*

c) *Karma*

I AM SMART UNLESS I AM REALLY, REALLY IN LOVE,

AND THEN I AM RIDICULOUSLY STUPID.

TAYLOR SWIFT

In 2017, Taylor launched an app
called The Swift Life which offered
users the latest updates on her life,
as well as the ability to interact with
each other and even Taylor herself!
Users could also access exclusive
material, including "Taymojis",
which were Taylor's own brand of
emoji stickers. Unfortunately, the
app was discontinued in 2019.

In the *Red* track "Starlight", where did the speaker meet Bobby?

_____

a) at a yacht club party

c) on the boardwalk

c) at the beach

WE HAVE TO LIVE
BRAVELY IN ORDER
TO TRULY FEEL
ALIVE, AND THAT
MEANS NOT BEING
RULED BY OUR
GREATEST FEARS.

TAYLOR SWIFT

Taylor is a self-confessed Twihard and requested to star as an extra in the second *Twilight* movie, *New Moon*. Swifties have speculated that the track "Haunted" was actually inspired by the franchise, and that the speaker is Bella Swan.

How long did it take
Taylor to write the
song "Love Story"?

_____

a) 20 minutes

b) an hour

c) a week

Anytime someone tells me that I can't do something, I want to do it more.

TAYLOR SWIFT

Super Bowl 2024 attracted
123.4 million viewers, making it not
only the most watched Super Bowl of
all time, but the second most watched
TV programme in history! (The Apollo
11 moon landing takes top place.)
Commentators have attributed
this to Taylor Swift's presence
at the game as she attended to
support her partner, Travis Kelce.

Which state was
Taylor born in?

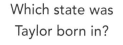

a) New York

b) Tennessee

c) Pennsylvania

IF YOU GO TOO
FAR DOWN THE
RABBIT HOLE OF
WHAT PEOPLE

THINK ABOUT YOU,
IT CAN CHANGE
EVERYTHING ABOUT
WHO YOU ARE.

TAYLOR SWIFT

DID YOU KNOW...

The track "Speak Now" is said to have been inspired by one of Taylor's best friends, Hayley Williams, and her experience of attending the wedding of her ex-boyfriend and former Paramore bandmate, Josh Farro. Taylor allegedly asked Hayley whether she would object and "speak now".

What is the background
visual for the lyric video to the
evermore track "dorothea"?

---

a) bleachers at a
sports stadium

b) a billboard

c) fields of grass

LOVE IS THE
ONE WILD CARD.

TAYLOR SWIFT

DID
YOU
KNOW...

Taylor was the first Saturday
Night Live host to write their own
monologue. The monologue is
usually prepared by the in-house
writers, but Taylor scripted it
herself, creating the now-iconic
"Monologue Song (La La La)".

In the *folklore* track "the last great american dynasty", what colour did Rebekah dye her neighbour's dog?

———

a) pink

b) green

c) maroon

Be yourself,
chase your
dreams and
just never
say never.

TAYLOR SWIFT

DID YOU KNOW...

Taylor wrote the track "Crazier",
which appeared on the soundtrack
to *Hannah Montana: The Movie*.
She even had her own cameo in the
film and can be seen performing
the song in the barn dance scene.

Taylor treated Swifties to not one, not two, but *three* remixes of the *evermore* track "willow". Which of the following is *not* the name of a remix?

___

a) "sad witch version"

b) "lonely witch version"

c) "dancing witch version"

I FEEL JEALOUSY, BUT I'VE BEEN TRYING TO CHANNEL IT

INTO MUTUAL ADMIRATION AND INSPIRATION.

TAYLOR SWIFT

Although Taylor is best
known as a guitarist,
she can also play the piano,
the banjo and the ukulele.

When she was 12, Taylor sang the national anthem at a basketball game for which professional sports team?

_____

a) Memphis Grizzlies

b) Philadelphia 76ers

c) Chicago Bulls

SONGS FOR
ME ARE LIKE A
MESSAGE IN A
BOTTLE. YOU SEND
THEM OUT TO
THE WORLD, AND
MAYBE THE PERSON
WHO YOU FEEL
THAT WAY ABOUT
WILL HEAR ABOUT
IT SOMEDAY.

TAYLOR SWIFT

The "drum" that can be heard in the *1989* track "Wildest Dreams" is actually a recording of Taylor's own heartbeat. She felt that a heartbeat would capture the romantic themes of the track, and she even credited her heart on the personnel list.

During her Red Tour, Taylor dressed up as a circus performer to perform which song?

_____

a) "The Lucky One"

b) "We Are Never Ever Getting Back Together"

c) "22"

Happiness and confidence are the prettiest things you can wear.

TAYLOR SWIFT

When Taylor dated the actor Taylor Lautner after they met on the set of the ensemble romcom *Valentine's Day*, the paparazzi dubbed the couple "Taylor Squared". The pair remained on good terms following their split, with Taylor Lautner making a guest appearance in the music video for "I Can See You (Taylor's Version) (From the Vault)" over a decade later.

Which era is represented
by the bathroom in
the Lover House?

a) *1989*

b) *Reputation*

c) *Lover*

**PEOPLE ARE
GOING TO TALK
ABOUT YOU.**

**BUT MAYBE
YOU'RE HAVING
MORE FUN THAN
THEM ANYWAY.**

TAYLOR SWIFT

DID
YOU
KNOW...

Taylor enjoys a mini-marathon
of the sitcom *Friends* to unwind
after the adrenaline rush of
performing to a sold-out stadium.
Her recovery routine then consists
of a full day of rest where she
only leaves her bed to get food –
then returning to bed to eat it!

In the *Speak Now* track
"Mine", what time was
the couple's fight?

_____

a) 1.58 a.m.

b) 2.00 a.m.

c) 2.30 a.m.

SILENCE SPEAKS
SO MUCH LOUDER
THAN SCREAMING
TANTRUMS. NEVER
GIVE ANYONE AN
EXCUSE TO SAY
THAT YOU'RE CRAZY.

TAYLOR SWIFT

DID YOU KNOW...

Taylor modelled for Abercrombie & Fitch in their 2003 "Rising Stars" campaign! The hauntingly prescient photo features Taylor with her guitar, wiping away a tear – three years before the release of the ballad "Teardrops On My Guitar".

In the *Red* track "All Too Well", what item of clothing does Taylor leave behind?

---

a) her coat

b) her scarf

c) her hat

Maybe you aren't meant to fit in. Maybe you're meant to stand out.

TAYLOR SWIFT

DID YOU KNOW...

A rumour once spread that Taylor's legs were insured for a massive $40 million, should she ever sustain an injury that meant she couldn't perform. Taylor acknowledged the rumour by posting a photo of a scratch on her leg from her cat Meredith on Instagram, asking her to pay out the $40 million.

What is Taylor's
middle name?

a) Alison
b) Andrea
c) Marjorie

I DON'T COMPETE WITH OTHER PEOPLE IN THE INDUSTRY,

I COMPETE WITH MYSELF.

TAYLOR SWIFT

Taylor's talent for creative writing
was evident early on. When she was
only ten years old, she won a national
poetry contest with a poem entitled
"There's a Monster in My Closet".

What animal does Taylor
claim her spirit animal is?

_____

a) a cat

b) a fox

c) a butterfly

IF SOMEBODY
HURTS YOU, IT'S
OKAY TO CRY
A RIVER. JUST
REMEMBER TO
BUILD A BRIDGE
AND GET OVER IT.

TAYLOR SWIFT

Taylor's earliest publicized
relationship was with singer-
songwriter Joe Jonas... who allegedly
broke up with her over a 27-second
phone call. The messages in Taylor's
CD lyric booklets have confirmed
that the trilogy "Forever & Always",
"Last Kiss" and "Holy Ground"
was inspired by this relationship.

How many reasons does Taylor say she could give Stephen for choosing her in the *Fearless* track "Hey Stephen"?

_____

a) 10

b) 50

c) 100

I think the
perfection of
love is that it's
not perfect.

TAYLOR SWIFT

DID
YOU
KNOW...

Taylor has written under the
pseudonym Nils Sjöberg. She wrote
"This Is What You Came For",
the Calvin Harris track featuring
Rihanna, at her piano and even
provided the backing vocals.

In which show did Taylor
make her acting debut?

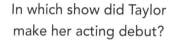

a) *CSI*

b) *Bones*

c) *Law & Order*

I THINK THAT
BEING FEARLESS
IS HAVING A
LOT OF FEARS,

BUT YOU JUMP
ANYWAY.

TAYLOR SWIFT

Taylor was made into a waxwork
at the Madame Tussauds gallery in
Hollywood in 2015. She also became
a permanent fixture at Madame
Tussauds London on 13 December
2019, Taylor's thirtieth birthday.

Taylor is known for hosting dinner parties and making baked goods. Which sweet treat does she always make in the fall?

———

a) chai sugar cookies

b) pumpkin spice cupcakes

c) apple cinnamon rolls

THE LESSON I'VE
LEARNED THE MOST
OFTEN IN LIFE
IS THAT YOU'RE
ALWAYS GOING
TO KNOW MORE IN
THE FUTURE THAN
YOU KNOW NOW.

TAYLOR SWIFT

DID
YOU
KNOW...

Taylor's eleventh studio album, *The Tortured Poets Department*, broke the all-time record for most streamed album in a single day, surpassing 300 million Spotify streams when it was released on 19 April 2024. Once again, history was made!

What did Taylor name
the giant inflatable snake
that appeared on the
Reputation World Tour?

_____

a) Kim

b) Karyn

c) Kanye

Just be
yourself,
there is no
one better.

TAYLOR SWIFT

FINAL WORD

Now you've experienced this powerful dose of fearless words from the woman herself, as well as insights into Taylor's creativity and resilience, you too are well on your way to dreaming big, shaking off the haters and stepping into your power.

Return to this little book whenever you need more Taylor in your life and open on any page to spark your Swiftie joy.

ANSWERS

8. c	47. b
11. b	50. b
14. c	53. b
17. c	56. c
20. b	59. b
23. b	62. c
26. b	65. c
29. a	68. b
32. c	71. b
35. a	74. b
38. b	77. b
41. a	80. c
44. b	83. b

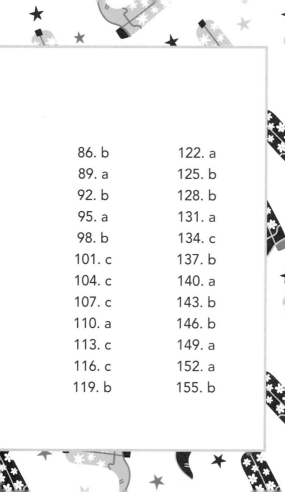

86. b	122. a
89. a	125. b
92. b	128. b
95. a	131. a
98. b	134. c
101. c	137. b
104. c	140. a
107. c	143. b
110. a	146. b
113. c	149. a
116. c	152. a
119. b	155. b

Have you enjoyed this book? If so, find us on Facebook at Summersdale Publishers, on Twitter/X at @Summersdale and on Instagram and TikTok at @summersdalebooks and get in touch. We'd love to hear from you!

www.summersdale.com

IMAGE CREDITS

Cover image and throughout – Taylor Swift © Joci Sampaio/Shutterstock.com; p.2 and throughout – sunglasses © ALEXOM11/Shutterstock.com; p.5 – microphone © Tartila/Shutterstock.com; p.6 and throughout – guitar © Vilmos Varga/Shutterstock.com; p.8 and throughout – cowboy boots © kenyaa/Shutterstock.com; p.12 and throughout – lips © Nadya_Art/Shutterstock.com; p.20 and throughout – cat © KittyVector/Shutterstock.com